FOOD FORTRESS

Jonathan Lever   www.archilever.com

ENDING WORLD HUNGER

FOOD FORTRESS

… ending world hunger..

I like the name / title for the book, food fortress… as it conjures up the feeling of something well protected, difficult to break past, well defended, well guarded, strong, resilient. And this is how the worlds food security and access to food for all should be – a well guarded protected situation of sorts. And quite simply put, this is where we should be by now in 2022. But its far from the case – not just in developing countries, but definitely in so called developed countries.

A lot has changed over the past two decades, and right back in the 1980s, through the 90s there was in international magazines and media, and the term 3rd world, or developing countries thrown around quite a bit – but I think in many respects those terms or definitions are completely irrelevant today – it really depends on what you're using as a yard stick to measure the worlds values and issues today. Because there are millions of homeless, hungry people in the USA as there are in the U. K – so levels of hunger are present in supposedly top tier countries. In fact in many ways with more access to land in developing countries there is greater food security, and certainly far better potential for good food security if handled correctly.

We live in a very materialistic world, there is absolutely no doubt about that – materialistic to the point of utter stupidity at times. People literally camping outside shops for days, and certainly all night to get the latest apple phone or some other ridiculous gadget they want – because a new model is coming out. We are a heavily consumerized world these days, where more and more emphasis is on things, and gadgets and people seem to live on phones. Priorities on world affairs, things which used to be normal are changing – its expected, as the world evolves of course.

Despite all these fancy gadgets and technology, and access to information, the relationship between this more and more competitive, materialistic world and gigantic over urbanisation we have witnessed in the past 25 years especially, has come with problems. Cities have swelled in size and numbers of people as never seen before. The access to information is supposedly greater than ever, yet there are a number of key factors which are bubbling away in the background, which I think are growing, not decreasing.

You would be horribly mistaken in thinking that food insecurity is a problem in some developing country only – right in the middle of well developed countries cities there is food insecurity – for different reasons, but it exists. The reasons across the world range from access to costs. You can still be in a city with plenty of food outlets but still have lots of people unable to afford it – which is often the case in big cities. As cities pile up with more and more people, we are seeing many vertical slums being created, and we are seeing big cities start creating poverty from high costs vrs salaries.

Certainly in many US cities and in the UK the number of food insecure people is staggering. Government food hand outs and benefits packages run into the many millions just in the UK. Then of course you have delightful situations like we saw in Venezuela, when you have massive amounts of people crammed into a large sprawling city and as the economy tanks, you see people in a highly urbanised concrete jungle finding themselves without food and rummaging through bins, and shops empty.

So cities always have that intrinsic danger of when there is some kind of stupid government event like locking up the public over covid and crashing their jobs, or general economic decline – if you're in a built up city, you're buggered on the food front

I believe that all big cities have this same trap, or potential trap, in that when the economy goes pear shaped, or there is some kind of rogue government, or inflation or whatever the case may be – if you have large populations unable to grow their own food – you will at some stage get problems – there could be even things such as currency drops, fuel supply problems, war, border blockades etc etc -the list goes on really. But for a country, energy self sufficiency and food and water supply are just the basics really.

The extensive urbanisation over the years has in effect disconnected people from land to grow food. But even where there is land, the overall thinking around the world needs to shift up a few gears to look at the problem of food security from a worldwide perspective.

I know there are many great farmers, many great food and tree planting initiatives – many, too many to count really…BUT…the world is a big place and populations will grow and I think that with a very simple concept of turning the world into a place where readily available natural food is in surplus supply can only be a good thing.

With such a materialistic world, there have never been so many things to buy out there as you can right now. You can just hope onto the likes of Amazon and start ordering pretty much anything. But what about free food. Most things have a price tag, and why not of course, as they've taken someone or people, or a factory or a company, time and resources and costs to make or supply – but in nature – things are for free. This is the big difference. You don't have to pay an avocado tree to grow. You don't have to pay an orange or mango tree to grow. Provided the seed is planted, it does the rest. Pretty much anyway.

So what am I talking about here in general terms for free food – and ending world hunger.

Well the concept is really simple. I believe that if the world and the world governments made a ten year plan to aggressively plant all kinds of trees for food surplus, everywhere its possible not connected to some profiteer, then things could radically change. So lets look at some examples.. Lets take the avocado tree. Avocados are pretty much as super food – they literally have everything in them – all the vitamins and minerals you could hope for – they really are a super food. So if people were to drop used seeds back at collection points and a government programme with staff and or volunteers were planting avocado trees daily in ten years time trees providing a superfood would be everywhere.
All the road edges, parks, fields ,school fields and green spaces, could be edged with avocado trees, mango trees, orange trees, macadamia nut trees etc etc etc.

If the countries around the world aimed for a billion avocado trees to be planted, and a billion of each of the other trees, then in one generation there would be food surplus everywhere – and enough to feed all the animals, birds etc etc. If every road edge was lined with a mixture of fruit and nut trees, one would be able to go outside and at least not starve. Kids at all schools could eat mostly for free. And its all healthy too.

Why are we so stupid as humans that this is not already happening – why are we going to vegetable and fruit markets, when this stuff should be growing everywhere and you can simple go outside and pick whatever you want. If one has to take the whole range of nuts, berries, fruits, avocados, etc etc, have them growing everywhere you could to a large degree eat for free off nature.

Humans are the only animal on the planet that pays for food. In fact pays for anything. Humans are supposed to have the greatest minds – yet we can even sort out food security. The solution here is actually very simple and no one should be going hungry in any country, ever really – there is no need. Why have cities been developed without this integrated food surplus aspect built into them – these seemingly stupid decisions just don't seem right.

Nature provides a full range of free food options, carrying all the vitamins and minerals we need – yet we are buying processed food, food full of preservatives, colouring etc etc. We go into supermarkets and its normal to be paying vast sums of money for fruit – its actually total madness – when you stand back and look at the earth, and the diversity of trees providing food, yet there is pretty much no evidence of them in cities –what are we thinking humans ??!! How can we have let such simple obvious basic things fall by the wayside – none of this makes any sense.

Sure we need farmers, there will always be a need for commercial farming for food supply and commercial quantities of many food types, but it just makes sense to get some of these basics right, and there is nothing to loose in planting all these food related trees either. I'm not saying these planting exercises will mean that you wont need supermarkets for food, of course you will, but by having a huge food surplus just growing everywhere, it does meant that no one should ever go hungry, or be unhealthily hungry either. And of course cold weather climate countries will be more limited in this, but so be it – there are plenty of other countries that are quite capable of growing pretty much anything. If I were being cynical, it looks like cities have been deliberately planned to create food insecurity the way they are planned and the lack of food supply.

You go into a supermarket, you pay for olives, bananas, dates, oranges, mangos, lemons, tomatoes, cucumbers, egg plant, all kinds of nuts, vegetables, all kinds of fruits –the list goes on – where as you should be able to walk down any street and pick things for free. Why else were food bearing trees and plants put on the earth. Because they certainly weren't put on the earth so that only people cant eat in cities and pay huge sums of money to buy things that should be free – as they are free from nature – this is just madness.

You don't walk outside and pay for sunshine – you don't walk outside to some parking meter and pay for sun, or rain, or wind, or trees, or birds, or animals, or plants – they should all be there naturally in abundance. At what point did people think it was a smart idea to limit what nature has provided for free. And hunger and starvation and food insecurity is nothing new here either. Its been going on throughout history – just like stupid wars. So we have leadership problems clearly – and the exclusion of nature – ie: fruit trees, nuts etc from public interfaces and planning and provision is just unacceptable really – there are no good excuses either.

What are the basics for a human – food shelter, sunlight, heat… Well I believe that food is a human right to a certain extent because nature provides it for free – why are fruit trees not everywhere. I think there is far too much control emerging in cities, too much control over stupid things like a parking violations and a million other petty things, but we cant even get food supply right. And it will save people lots of money in the process. The weekly food costs on fruits and vegetables and nuts for a family are quite high in any city – they shouldn't be.

Every school yard, should have plenty of nutrition growing for free and be planned into every school development really. It just common sense really isn't it. IF road edges became food edges, that too would make sense.

Just look at the tree above – talk about nature giving back. See how many oranges are growing on that tree – and bear in mind that every orange is filled with more seeds for plenty more trees. Each orange tree probably has enough seeds for 500 new trees easily. Conservatively. And this is the joy of nature, it gives back – why cant we learn from the very basics of nature, but instead humans are greedy. Every fruit gives back. And even if its like and avocado tree, if you add up all the avocados from one tree in a season, you looking and hundreds of new trees from each tree potentially. Nature is a giver. Things created on this earth give back – for free too. We don't need to commercialise everything on the planet for profit, while people starve on the streets or are not getting the right nutrition because of costs.

The avocado just on its own is a superfood

One decent sized avocado is a meal for a kid

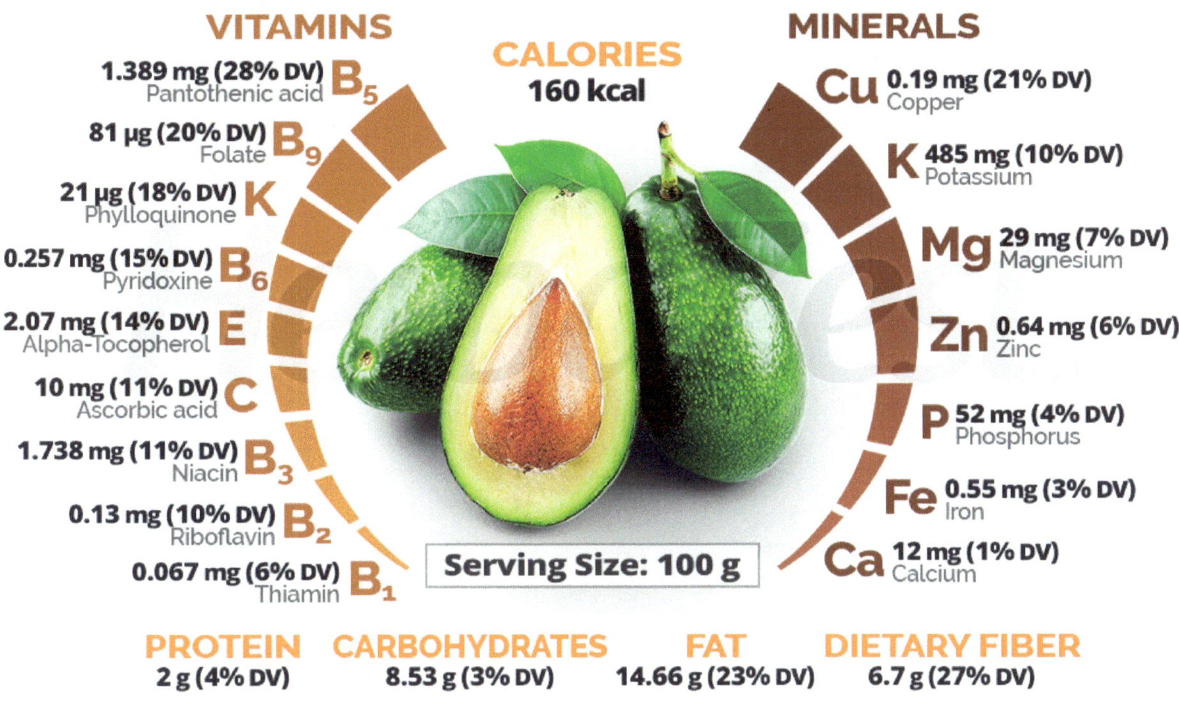

The avocado is a good example, thus going to highlight it here mainly just to show the value of just one item. Just one of these a day plus a glass of milk is enough to keep a kid going all day. They really are like a wonder food – a whole meal in one. So just even with these growing everywhere, where the public have these in abundance would stop people going hungry and give you the right minerals and vitamins you need to keep you going through the day. The power of nature is quite evident in just the avocado. But there are hundreds of other fruits and nuts etc etc which when used in combination per day would rally provide all you need year round. And with billions of these trees planted everywhere around human settlements across the world, we are already onto a good thing.

Fresh Avocado (5 oz. medium size)	1 serving of avocado About 1/5 of an avocado 1 oz. (30g)	% Daily Value	1.25 serving About ¼ of an avocado 1.25 oz. (37.5g)	2.5 servings About ½ of an avocado 2.5 oz. (75g)	5 servings About 1 whole avocado 5 oz. (150g)
Calories	50		60	130	250
Total Fat (g)	4.5	7% DV	6	12	23
Sat Fat (g)	0.5	3% DV	1	2	3
Trans Fat (g)	0.0		0	0	0
Polyunsaturated Fat (g)	0.5		1	1	3
Monounsaturated Fat (g)	3.0		4	7	15
Cholesterol (mg)	0.0	0% DV	0	0	0
Sodium (mg)	0.0	0% DV	0	5	10
Potassium (mg)	150.0	4% DV	190	380	760
Total Carbohydrate (g)	3.0	1% DV	3	6	13
Dietary Fiber (g)	2.0	8% DV	3	5	10
Sugars (g)	0.0		0	0	0
Protein (g)	0.0		1	1	3

VITAMINS

	1 serving of avocado About 1/5 of an avocado 1 oz. (30g)	% Daily Value	1.25 serving About ¼ of an avocado 1.25 oz. (37.5g)	2.5 servings About ½ of an avocado 2.5 oz. (75g)	5 servings About 1 whole avocado 5 oz. (150g)
Folate (mcg or µg)	27	6% DV	33.8	67.5	135
Niacin (mg)	0.6	2% DV	0.7	1.4	2.9
Pantothenic Acid (mg)	0.4	4% DV	0.5	1.1	2.2
Riboflavin (mg)	0.0	4% DV	0.1	0.1	0.2
Vitamin A (IU)	44	1% DV	55	110	220
Vitamin B6 (mg)	0.1	4% DV	0.1	0.2	0.4
Vitamin C (mg)	2.6	4% DV	3.3	6.5	13
Vitamin E (IU)	0.9	4% DV	1.1	2.2	4.4

MINERALS

	1 serving of avocado About 1/5 of an avocado 1 oz. (30g)	% Daily Value	1.25 serving About ¼ of an avocado 1.25 oz. (37.5g)	2.5 servings About ½ of an avocado 2.5 oz. (75g)	5 servings About 1 whole avocado 5 oz. (150g)
Calcium (mg)	4	0% DV	5	10	20
Copper (mg)	0.1	2% DV	0.1	0.1	0.3
Iron (mg)	0.2	2% DV	0.2	0.5	0.9
Magnesium (mg)	9	2% DV	11.3	22.5	45
Manganese (mg)	0.0	2% DV	0.1	0.1	0.2
Phosphorous (mg)	16	2% DV	20	40	80
Zinc (mg)	0.2	0% DV	0.3	0.5	1.0

Avocados are super easy to grow as well from the seed – and therefore even school kids can easily have fun and participate in the populating the world with avocados. It would be a good thing if kids were all involved in agriculture basics at junior school anyway

Planning cities with proper greenbelts and wildlife for the future..

Cities should have proper greenbelts that run through with plants, trees, water and teaming with wildlife – and importantly with food producing trees and plants

Planning cities with proper greenbelts and wildlife for the future..with plenty of food producing trees

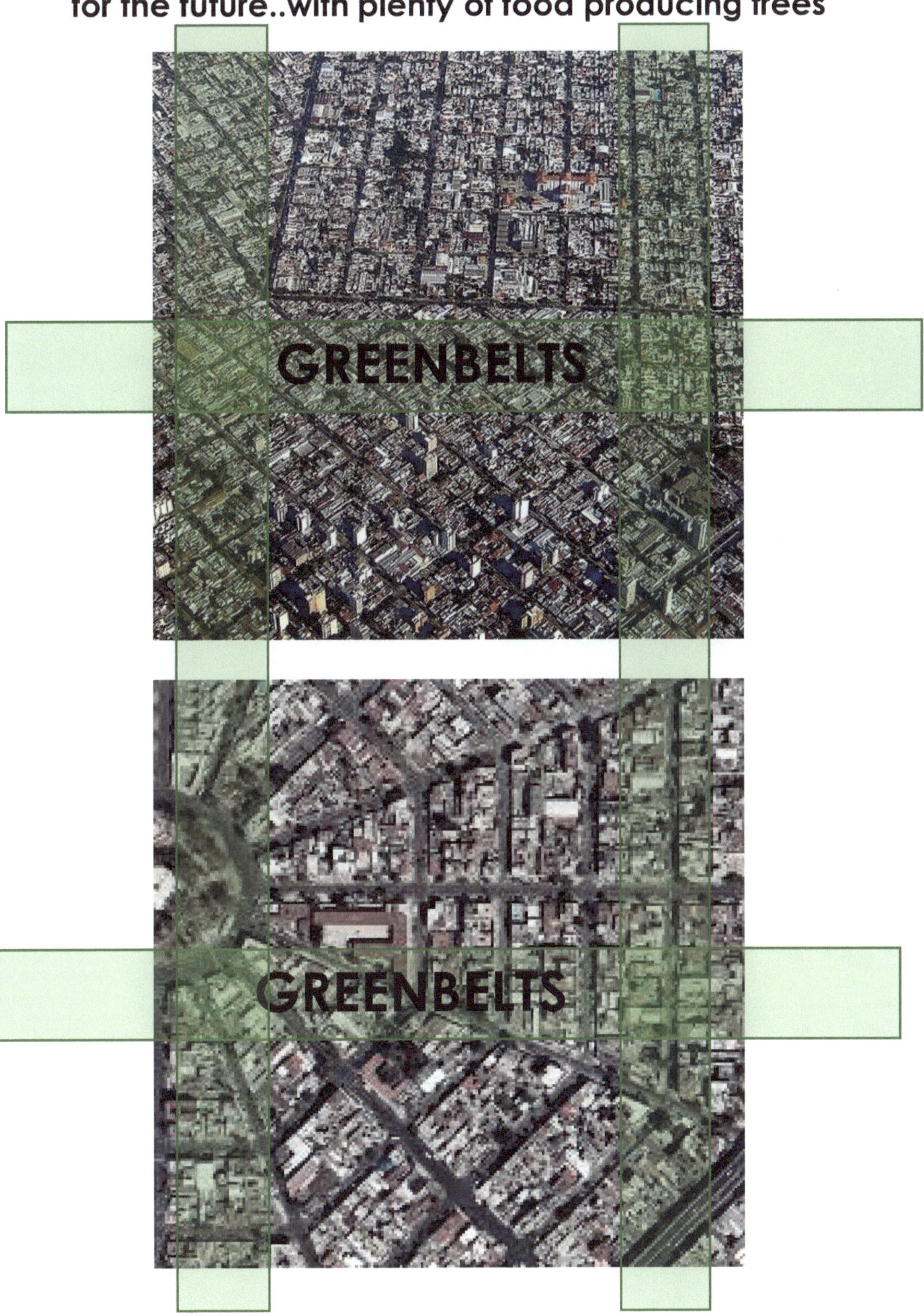

Proper flowing integrated green areas filled with wildlife and food bearing trees and plants

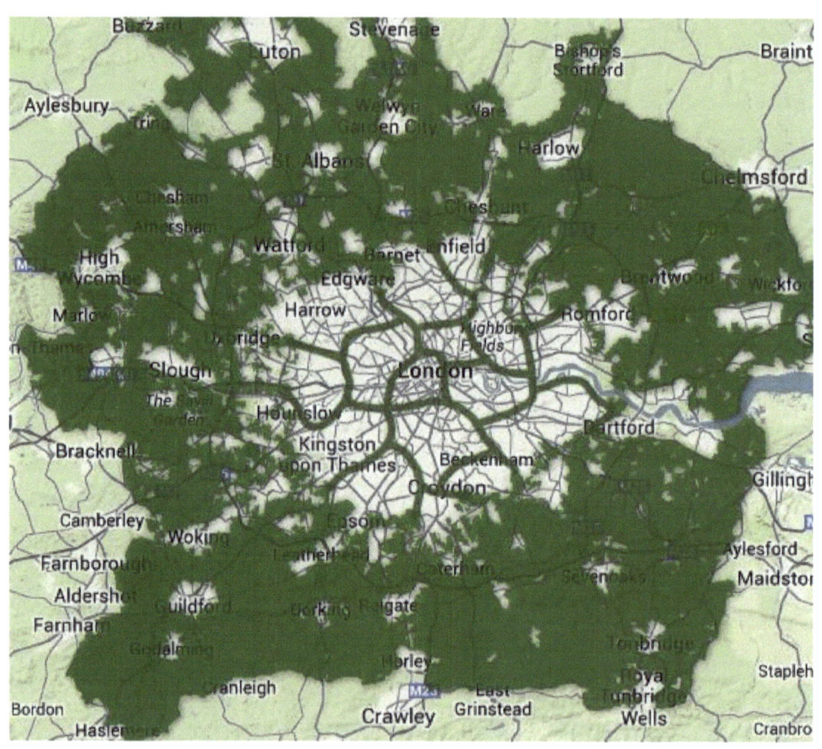

The images I have used are just a tiny insert really in the bigger picture. You could do entire books just on the different types of free food provided by nature. The range is vast – as especially as the world is now connected so in many ways things aren't as exotic as they might have been in the past, as interchanging seeds and plants between countries is really easy to do. So there really is little excuse for this not happening on a large scale – in as many public areas as possible – so people can get free food.

It really isn't rocket science. This little book is really just another prod towards this happening that's all. There are plenty of books on how to grow any kind of tree and plant you can think of. Very detailed ones in fact, but when you start looking at the big over urbanisation we are seeing today, the lack of free food options is alarming. And city scape like these are as close to hell as you're going to get really – and how on earth can fruit bearing trees be put to work in sensibly with these kind of economic slave complexes

Hell on earth – no food anywhere near

Hell on earth – no food anywhere near